Eugène Delacroix/Édouard Manet

THE COMPLETE ILLUSTRATIONS FROM

Delacroix's "Faust" and Manet's "The Raven"

Edited and with an Introduction by
Breon Mitchell
Chairman, Department of Comparative Literature,
Indiana University

THE LILLY LIBRARY OF INDIANA UNIVERSITY, BLOOMINGTON
In Association With
DOVER PUBLICATIONS, INC., NEW YORK

Published in Canada by General Publishing Company, Ltd., 30
Lesmill Road, Don Mills, Toronto, Ontario.
Published in the United Kingdom by Constable and Company,
Ltd., 10 Orange Street, London WC2H 7EG.

This Dover edition, first published in 1981, in association with
the Lilly Library of Indiana University, Bloomington, contains:
(1) All the illustrations and a few text pages from *Faust, tragédie
de M. de Goethe, . . . Ornée . . . de dix-sept dessins . . . par M. Eugène
Delacroix*, originally published by Ch[arles] Motte, Paris, 1828 (com-
plete title page reproduced in the present volume).
(2) The complete text and illustrations of *Le Corbeau / The Raven
/ poëme par Edgar Poe . . . avec illustrations par Édouard Manet*, orig-
inally published by Richard Lesclide, Paris, 1875 (complete title
page reproduced in the present volume).
(3) New material written specially for the present edition by
Breon Mitchell: Introduction; Notes on the Plates for *Faust*; Notes
on the Plates for *The Raven*.

International Standard Book Number: 0-486-24127-0
Library of Congress Catalog Card Number: 80-71100

Manufactured in the United States of America
Dover Publications, Inc.
180 Varick Street
New York, N.Y. 10014

THE COMPLETE ILLUSTRATIONS FROM

Delacroix's "Faust" and Manet's "The Raven"

Introduction

THE PRESENT VOLUME unites for the first time two of the great landmarks of nineteenth-century book illustration. Delacroix's *Faust* (1828) has often been considered the first of the truly modern *livres d'artiste*, "a profession of faith by the new school of artists—comparable to the Preface to *Cromwell* for the field of French Romantic literature" (Henri Béraldi), while the collaboration of Manet and Mallarmé for *The Raven* (1875) stands as a masterpiece of later nineteenth-century book production, in which many of the dominant tendencies of twentieth-century art are clearly evident.

These two books are comparable in many ways: each consists of a text by a foreign author who seemed to speak to the spirit of the age; each was illustrated with original lithographs by a major artist whose reputation was primarily that of a painter; each was produced with the utmost care for fine printing. Yet, for various reasons, both were commercial failures. These pioneering efforts were not in vain, however, for they now stand as truly distinguished forerunners of a new artistic genre.

The *livre d'artiste* differs from the traditional illustrated book in several respects. The illustrations are, in each case, original works of art (woodcuts, lithographs, etchings, engravings) executed by the artist himself and printed under his supervision. The book thus contains original works of art and not simply reproductions. This limits the number of copies that can be produced: such books are normally published in editions of less than three hundred copies (240 for *The Raven*) and are often extremely expensive. As a result, the series as a whole may well remain unknown to the general public. The present volume contains the complete set of plates for each book, together with text that reveals the relationship of word and image in the original. In the case of *Faust*, only a few sample text pages are supplied. In the case of *The Raven* it has been possible to reproduce the entire book from cover to cover. The copies utilized are those in the collection of the Lilly Library of Indiana University, Bloomington, Indiana, and the photographic reproductions have been made from the originals. The portrait of Goethe and Plates 2–6, 8–10, 14, 16 and 17 from *Faust* are identical in size to the originals; the remaining plates have been only slightly reduced. The text

pages and plates for *The Raven* are approximately three-fourths of their original size.

DELACROIX AND FAUST

In June of 1825, Eugène Delacroix was in London, sampling the intellectual life and the night life by turns. On the 18th of that month, he wrote to his friend J.-P. Pierret:

> I saw here a play about Faust which is the most diabolical thing imaginable. The Mephistopheles is a masterpiece of character and intelligence. It is an adaptation of Goethe's *Faust*; the principal elements are retained. They have made it into an opera with a mixture of broad comedy and some extremely sinister effects. The scene in the church is played with priests singing and distant organ music. Theatrical effect can go no further. (*Selected Letters*, trans. Jean Stewart. London: Eyre & Spottiswoode, 1971)

As this letter reveals, *Faust* was already well known to Delacroix. As early as 1821 he had been "rather struck" by a series of line engravings for the play by Moritz von Retzsch, and he was thoroughly familiar with the French version by Gérard de Nerval. From the beginning it was the figure of Mephistopheles that seized his imagination, personifying in his eyes a fundamental aspect of the Romantic genius. Yet, as with Faust, two souls lived within his breast. Tormented by "accesses of moral suffering" as well as by "sadness and boredom," he seemed to see in Faust a reflection of his own moral dilemmas as an artist. As Louvre curator René Huyghe has said, "Faust was in tune with the anguish that Delacroix shared with the Romantics, and the key to which he was seeking. The encounter between Faust and Mephistopheles fitted in with his passionate interest in dualism and conflict too marvelously well for him not to be obsessed by it."

In the year following his return from England, Delacroix began the now-famous series of prints illustrating Goethe's text. He chose as a medium a relatively recently invented process called lithography, which allowed the artist to work directly upon the stone and to produce a velvety black texture

FAUST,

TRAGÉDIE DE M. DE GOETHE,

TRADUITE EN FRANÇAIS

PAR M. ALBERT STAPFER,

Ornée d'un Portrait de l'Auteur,

ET DE DIX-SEPT DESSINS COMPOSÉS D'APRÈS LES PRINCIPALES SCÈNES DE L'OUVRAGE ET EXÉCUTÉS SUR PIERRE

PAR M. EUGÈNE DELACROIX.

A PARIS,

CHEZ CH. MOTTE, ÉDITEUR,

Imprimeur-Lithographe de LL. AA. RR. Mgr le Duc d'Orléans et Mgr le Duc de Chartres,

RUE DES MARAIS N° 13;

ET CHEZ SAUTELET, LIBRAIRE,

PLACE DE LA BOURSE.

M DCCC XXVIII.

Fig. 1. Original title page of the Delacroix *Faust.*

that was admirably suited to the abundant night scenes of *Faust*. Delacroix seemed to instinctively understand the possibilities of the medium and achieved effects which, for their time, were unique. The publisher Charles Motte suggested that the series should be issued together with a translation of the play by Albert Stapfer. In later years, Delacroix professed to have been dissatisfied with this idea, which he felt hurt the sales of his own work; nevertheless, the fact that the illustrations were issued in book form, and not simply as a suite of lithographs (as was the case later with Delacroix's illustrations to *Hamlet*), was of immense importance. In its final form, Delacroix's *Faust* was to become one of the earliest books in France illustrated by lithography, and represented the true beginning of Romantic illustration as well. As David Bland has pointed out, "All [previous efforts] pale beside Delacroix's *Faust* . . . it marks the beginning of the great French tradition of the painter-lithographer. . . . True, many great painters illustrated books in the eighteenth century, but they never prepared their own printing surfaces." The freedom and spontaneity that could be achieved by working directly on the stone clearly appealed to Delacroix's nature, and the results found equal favor in the eyes of Goethe himself.

By the 1820s, Goethe was almost a legend; along with Byron and Shakespeare, he was one of the great sources of Romantic inspiration for the age. He was well aware of Delacroix's work while it was still in progress, and upon seeing two of the plates (a Walpurgis Night scene and Auerbach's cellar) he was moved to remark to his friend Johann Peter Eckermann:

> One must acknowledge that this M. Delacroix has a great talent, which in *Faust* has found its true nourishment. The French public reproach him for an excess of savage force, but actually it is perfectly suitable here. He will, I hope, go all through *Faust*, and I anticipate a special pleasure from the witches' kitchen and the scene on the Brocken. We can see he has a good knowledge of life, for which a city like Paris has given him ample opportunity. And if I must confess that M. Delacroix has, in some scenes, surpassed my own notions, how much more will the reader find all in full life, and surpassing his imagination.

Such favorable responses from the author himself must have served as a welcome encouragement to the artist, and by 1827 a complete set of the plates seems to have been in Goethe's hands. The book was delayed, however, by various factors, including the publisher's desire for a frontispiece portrait of the author (see the notes below). Delacroix was also hard at work on one of his major paintings, *Sardanapalus*, which was to be exhibited in the Salon of 1827. At last, after a delay of some two years, the book appeared (Fig. 1).

Critics on all sides rushed to deride the results, which so clearly flew in the face of Neoclassical conventions. As Delacroix himself was later to remark: "The peculiar character of the illustrations themselves invited caricature and confirmed my reputation as one of the leaders of the *school of ugliness*. Gérard, however, although an academician, complimented me on some of the drawings, particularly that of

the tavern." Goethe remained a staunch admirer of the illustrations as well, and in a later conversation with Eckermann he enlarged upon the themes which he felt had fascinated the artist:

> *Faust* is a work which passes from heaven to earth, from the possible to the impossible, from the gross to the exquisite; all the antitheses which the play of bold imagination can create are there brought together; this is why Monsieur Delacroix felt at home in it . . . as though among his own family.

Over time, critics and art historians have placed Delacroix's illustrations more firmly within their historical context, stressing "the remarkable degree to which they stand apart from their probable antecedents" and, while recognizing their often uneven quality, discovering in them a power "which somehow manages to suggest those brilliant enigmas, those startling and dramatic contradictions, that make Goethe's play an appealing but elusive masterpiece" (Frank Trapp). In the final analysis it is worth recalling as well that Delacroix's *Faust* exhibits a somewhat deceptive sense of the world-wise and world-weary artist's sensibility. When the book appeared in 1828, the translator, Albert Stapfer, was 26; Delacroix had just turned 30.

MANET AND THE RAVEN

It was almost fifty years before another publisher contemplated a work comparable in importance to Delacroix's *Faust*. In 1874, Richard Lesclide contracted for a bilingual edition of Edgar Allan Poe's *The Raven*, to be illustrated by Édouard Manet and translated by Stéphane Mallarmé. In some ways it seemed as if history were repeating itself: like Delacroix, Manet was an anti-establishment artist whose paintings had scandalized the public and horrified the critics. Like Goethe, Poe was an author whose works appealed to the very center of a new sensibility. The publication of *The Raven* in 1875 was thus a statement of avant-garde literary and artistic taste, and its critical reception was eagerly awaited by poets and artists alike. Once again, however, the experiment proved to be a commercial failure, and the publisher never dared to embark on another such venture. Twenty-five years ahead of its time in concept and design, *The Raven* had nonetheless opened the door into the twentieth century.

One of the most appealing aspects of *The Raven* was the testimony it bore to the friendship of two men. Manet had first met Mallarmé sometime in 1873, and they soon became constant companions, regularly sharing their views on art and life until Manet's death in 1883. When a long-planned volume of Mallarmé's translations of Poe's poetry appeared at last in 1888, it bore the following dedication: "To the memory of Édouard Manet, these pages which we read together."

From their first meeting, Mallarmé had championed the art of Manet, defending him, for example, against the common criticism that he understood nothing of perspective and the

Fig. 2. Original front wrapper of the 1828 *Faust* (by Achille Devéria).

Fig. 3. Original back wrapper of the 1828 *Faust* (by Achille Devéria).

laws of design: "If we turn to natural perspective (not that utterly and artificially classic science which makes our eyes the dupes of a civilized education, but rather that artistic perspective which we learn from the extreme East—Japan, for example) and look at these seascapes of Manet, where the water at the horizon rises to the height of the frame, which alone interrupts it, we feel a new delight at the recovery of a long obliterated truth." Or, when the age-old demand of the academy for "finish" (against which Delacroix chafed in completing the portrait of Goethe) was repeatedly raised, Mallarmé was quick to ask, "Why is a work called unfinished when all its elements are in accord and it casts a spell that could easily be broken by an additional touch?"

Like Baudelaire before him, Mallarmé had also encouraged artists to turn their attention to the contemporary world, and Manet was proud to be among those who did. But, as Anne Coffin has pointed out, Mallarmé "admitted that he learned much from Manet's ability to saturate himself in his own observations and to extract the essential qualities from the world of multiple forms." Thus Mallarmé could speak of his own aim "to paint not the thing, but the effect that it produces. The truth must not therefore be made up of words, but of intentions, and the words are effaced before sensations."

The value of Manet's art had been recognized by other writers as well; both Baudelaire (whose passion for Poe was passed on to Mallarmé and Manet) and Zola had come to his defense in the 1860s. But it was Mallarmé, whose concern for the appearance of the printed page in relationship to word and image was far in advance of his time, who strove to unite the arts in a single physical object. It is in this sense that *The Raven* significantly advances the art of the book in the nineteenth century. Although, as in the case of *Faust*, the illustrations were printed *hors texte*, and thus did not affect the actual printed page as such, the integration of illustration and text is obviously central throughout; the resultant effect is striking.

Here is a book in which text and image are equally powerful, and carefully balanced. It is impossible to conceive of Manet and Mallarmé allowing the mood of the whole to be broken, as by the frontispiece in *Faust*. The gap in sensibility in this respect is nowhere more evident than in the covers of the two works. While Delacroix raised no objection at all to the vastly inferior cover decorations for *Faust* by Achille Devéria (Figs. 2 & 3), Manet exercised artistic control over even the color of the slip case: "My dear Lesclide," he wrote, "I am very much alarmed by the black silk which you plan to use as a cover. This would give the impression of a death notice. A parchment, a green paper, or one of delicate yellow, approximately the color [upon which] the frontispiece [is printed]: that is what we need. *Cordialités*. Éd. Manet."

In contrast to Delacroix, whose journal and letters provide us with a wealth of insights into the artist's thoughts, hopes and dreams, we know practically nothing of Manet's attitude toward his own work. He seems to have talked little about it and written less. Thus we cannot be sure of the extent to which he consciously set out to revitalize the art of his day, creating a vision in almost direct opposition to the accepted canons of the age. Today, it may still require a special effort on our part to recapture a sense of the striking originality of these illustrations in 1875—the boldness of abstraction, the sometimes startling perspectives, the assured power of the broken brushstrokes which set the mood in every plate. The implicit aesthetic is one that has turned away from the European tradition and the tyranny of the past, opening out toward the world and toward the future.

Notes on the Plates for "Faust"

Delacroix had been drawn to *Faust* principally by the figure of Mephistopheles, so it is perhaps not surprising that the Devil appears in thirteen of the seventeen plates; nor is the preponderance of night scenes (eight of them) unusual in a play steeped in a spiritual duality that often finds expression in terms of light and darkness. Yet an examination of the illustrations reveals other choices that are far from predictable.

Taken as a series, it is clear that the plates are carefully interrelated, creating not only a counterpart to the plot but also a reflection of the mood and imagery that imbue the drama. Three plates, for example, are devoted to individual portraits of the major characters, while yet another three are devoted to first encounters (Faust and the Devil, Faust and Gretchen, Gretchen and the Devil). The early plates of Wagner and Faust in the countryside are later balanced by those of Faust and Mephistopheles on the mountain. The recurrent emphasis on the setting sun in Plates 1, 4 and 11 reinforces visually a theme that may be less memorable in the text itself, and prepares the viewer for the symbolic significance of the light of dawn streaming into the window of the dungeon in the final plate, signaling Gretchen's escape from the powers of darkness. Delacroix's compositional arrangements serve similar purposes when, for example, Gretchen is shown caught between Faust and the Devil (Plate 8), while in the final plate it is Faust who is torn by the choice between her and Mephistopheles. On yet another level, the alternation of interior and exterior scenes is much more striking visually than verbally, and both the sense of stifling entrapment that overcomes Faust, and his longing for spiritual freedom, are powerfully conveyed. Gretchen's imprisonment in the dungeon thus serves as an ironic comment upon the contrast between physical and spiritual confinement. In yet other cases, visual echoes, such as the repeated depictions of the Devil leading Faust on (Plates 12, 14 and 17), reinforce the central themes of temptation, isolation, despair and hope. In such ways, Delacroix's illustrations become more than a simple retelling of *Faust* in pictures; they underline structural and symbolic parallels of importance to its total aesthetic effect.

NOTE: The French text consists of the translation of *Faust,*

Part One, which appeared in German in 1808. *Faust, Part Two* was published only after Goethe's death in 1832. When, in 1862, Delacroix was asked whether he had ever thought of illustrating the second part, he replied: "I was not acquainted with the *Second Faust*, and still knew it only superficially long after my plates were made. It seemed to me badly digested and not very interesting from the literary point of view, yet one of those works that are most appropriate to inspire painters by the mixture of characters and styles they permit. If the work had been more popular I might perhaps have undertaken it."

The quotations from *Faust* given in these notes are from a translation in progress by Philip Kimball. Though based directly on the German, they correspond to the French captions on the plates.

Frontispiece. PORTRAIT OF GOETHE.

This fine portrait, printed on China paper, was the cause of some dissatisfaction on the part of the artist. In a letter of October 1827, Delacroix wrote to his publisher Charles Motte: "I am very sorry for the hitch over the portrait. But it is extremely awkward for me to get it done. I simply have not the necessary time, I have my picture [*Sardanapalus*] to finish . . . and I shall be fully occupied for some time to come . . . it distresses me very much to see any further delay in the publication of a work which has been waiting about for two years already. . . . I am forced to admit my inadequacy in the matter of lithographic portraits, which always require a certain degree of finish." In spite of Delacroix's hesitation, the result gave little cause for complaint, although it is obviously at variance with the mood and style of the suite of illustrations that follows. A note at the end of the translator's introduction states that the frontispiece was copied from a sketch done in Weimar early in 1827, which Goethe had sent to the publisher for this purpose.

Plate 1. PROLOGUE IN HEAVEN. *(Opposite page 15 in the original edition.)*

> MEPHISTOPHELES:
> I like to see the old boy from time to time,
> And am careful not to break with him.
> It's very nice of such an important man
> To speak so humanly with the devil himself.

Delacroix opens with the Devil in his glory, flying over the medieval city. In the background the setting sun signals the alternation of "the light of paradise" with "deep and trembling night." The visual contrast of light and dark, day and night, continues throughout the book, and is a counterpart to the opposition of the respective powers of God and Mephistopheles. The totally contorted body of the Devil reflects his twisted nature; every joint is tensely angled, and both hands and feet end in sharply pointed nails. His muscular body, reflecting Delacroix's admiration for Michelangelo, rises on powerful wings. Yet the threat of the pointed church spires posed beneath him provides a striking image of the opposition of heaven and hell, and recalls the painful fall of Satan.

Plate 2.   NIGHT.   *(Opposite p. 24.)*

> Faust:
> Why are you grinning at me, hollow skull?
> Because your brain, like mine, once confusedly
> Sought out carefree days, and in the heavy gloom of
>   twilight,
> Longing for the truth, went wretchedly astray?

The sharp contrast this portrait of Faust offers to the first plate can hardly have been accidental. Delacroix introduces us to the protagonist alone at night in his study, contemplating a symbol of death. Faust is portrayed in an attitude of melancholy resignation. All the limbs of his body slump downward in total opposition to the bursting energy of Mephistopheles in flight. While the Devil enjoys the freedom of the heavens, Faust feels trapped in a "cursed, stifling hole-in-the-wall, / where even the light of heaven / comes but darkly through the stained-glass panes." The high-vaulted Gothic chamber in which he broods shows Delacroix's careful reading of the text. Faust's gaze soon moves from the "smouldering lamp" to the shelf above his head, where a phial of poison has long rested. Just as the goblet of poison is at his lips, the choral song of Easter morning reawakens his desire to live, and earth claims him once again.

Plate 3.   OUTSIDE THE CITY GATE.   *(Opposite p. 32.)*

> Faust:
> Oh, happy he who yet may hope
> To emerge from this sea of error . . .
> Alas, these spiritual wings will not
> So easily be matched by real wings.

Faust and Wagner rest from their stroll and look back upon the city. Here too we find the glow of the setting sun, as Faust reveals his longing to be lifted on wings above the earth like a god, "before me the day and behind me the night." That Delacroix recognized the textual link to Mephistopheles in flight is clear from the caption he chose for this plate. A new opposition is introduced as well, that of society and nature. Closely following the text, Delacroix includes a landscape in which "there are no flowers / instead [the sun] finds people in their finery" decorating the countryside. In the background "nimbly circling round and round / [the peasants] dance both left and right, / and set their cloaks in flight." The "lark lost in the blue space above," the mill on the horizon, the young couple and the plump citizen to the left, all are details taken from the text. Soon "the world has turned to gray, . . . and fog is falling," and it is time to return to the city.

Plate 4.   OUTSIDE THE CITY GATE.   *(Opposite p. 35.)*

> Wagner:
> See, a dog, and not a ghost is there.
> He growls and hesitates, crawls upon his belly,
> And wags his tail, like any dog.

As the sun sets in the background, Faust and Wagner are followed through the grain and stubble by a strange black dog, who will be transformed in the following scene into Mephistopheles himself. Although Wagner sees nothing unusual in the animal and simply appears amused, Faust is puzzled, particularly by a wisp of smoke curling near the animal's tail. Delacroix gives the reader a visual hint as to the dog's true nature: like Mephistopheles in flight, the animal is shown in an extremely contorted posture; moreover, the bulging eye of the Devil in Plate 1 is clearly reflected in the canine countenance. The fact that Wagner seems to have lost his beard and changed his cap since the previous plate is no doubt an oversight on the artist's part, and may indicate that there was a substantial interval of time between the execution of the two illustrations.

Plate 5.   FAUST'S STUDY. *(Opposite p. 38.)*

> Mephistopheles:
> Why all the noise? How may I be of service, my lord?

Once again it is night, and Faust has called forth the Devil from the dog that had followed him home. In their first confrontation, Faust rises excitedly, with his hand upon the New Testament, which he has been translating. The Devil's pose is dapper and self-assured, a stance which he maintains almost throughout the play. Faust soon enters into a pact with Mephistopheles and prepares to leave with him. Delacroix has carefully followed Goethe's description of Faust's study, although a different corner seems to be portrayed here from that in Plate 2. Thus we find books and papers piled on the floor in disorder, the old instruments of his father the alchemist, bottles and phials, and skulls. The small model skeleton hanging on the wall is Delacroix's invention, and may be intended as a visual premonition of the death of Gretchen's child.

Plate 6.   FAUST'S STUDY II. *(Opposite p. 51.)*

> Mephistopheles:
> Here too it's best to listen to but one,
> And swear by the master's word.
> In general: stick to words.
> Then you will enter into the temple of certainty
> Through the safest gate.

Delacroix has chosen to depict the scene in which the Devil dons Faust's clothing to fool a young prospective student. Here, as elsewhere in the illustrations, Delacroix heightens the dramatic tension by keeping all characters on stage at the same time (Goethe has Faust exit before the student enters). The play with clothing as costume clearly appealed to the visual sense of the artist, and his choice of caption implies a parallel to the reliance on words, or the surface of language, rather than substance. Faust is shown leaving the room to change for the journey with Mephistopheles. The Devil's sword still peeks out at Mephistopheles' side, while the innocent student carries only a quill and ink.

Plate 7.   AUERBACH'S CELLAR. *(Opposite p. 62.)*

> SIEBEL:
> Help! Fire! Help! Hell's on Fire! . . .
> Witchcraft! Go at him! The man is a criminal!

Seated in an attitude of amused superiority, the Devil watches as the wine that he has conjured up from holes bored in the tavern table changes to fire. Faust stands in the background, dressed as the Devil had instructed. The flames are "only a drop of Purgatory," to show Mephistopheles' power. Delacroix creates a scene of astonished motion in which the light from the flames effectively illuminates the faces and bodies of the men. As they are about to attack Mephistopheles with drawn daggers, he tames them easily by means of an hallucination.

Plate 8.   STREET. *(Opposite p. 73.)*

> FAUST:
> My fair young lady, may I dare
> To offer you my arm and company?

Under the influence of a love potion, Faust is irresistibly drawn to Gretchen (Margarete), whom he meets by chance in the street. She rejects him instantly: "I am neither fair, nor a lady, / And I can find my way home alone." As so often, Delacroix sums up a psychological moment in the position of the characters' bodies: the way in which Gretchen pushes Faust away with her elbow expresses a disdain equal to that on her face. She is, however, hemmed in between Faust and the Devil visually, as she soon will be in fact. In this street scene, Delacroix presents a wealth of architectural details from the medieval period.

Plate 8 is reproduced in the present volume facing the text page that it originally faced in the 1828 edition.

Plate 9.   THE NEIGHBOR'S HOUSE. *(Opposite p. 82.)*

> MEPHISTOPHELES:
> I've taken the liberty of simply coming in,
> For which I beg your pardon, ladies.

The first confrontation of Gretchen with the Devil recalls Plate 5, in which Mephistopheles introduces himself to Faust. Delacroix could hardly have contrasted the two scenes more sharply. Dapper and self-confident before Faust, the Devil here bows humbly, almost obsequiously, before the women. Leaning, as Faust was, upon the table, Gretchen is shown wearing the precious jewels that mysteriously appeared at her home. Once again, the role of surface appearance and costume assumes a visual importance. She does not realize that the Devil himself procured the jewels for Faust. Delacroix emphasizes the intermediary role of Martha, seated between Gretchen and the Devil, with her hands buried in the jewelry box.

Plate 10.   GRETCHEN'S ROOM. *(Opposite p. 99.)*

> GRETCHEN:
> Wherever he's not
> I've only a grave,
> And I've lost
> All joy in life.

Among the most famous scenes in Goethe's *Faust* is that of Gretchen at her spinning wheel. Delacroix utilizes this moment in the drama to offer a psychological portrait of the heroine. As he has done with Faust and the Devil, he portrays Gretchen alone. Her expression of sadness and melancholy matches the mood of the text. Her spindle has fallen to the floor, and the position of her body recalls the sense of tired resignation that seems to possess Faust in Plate 2. The half-hidden crucifix in the background, and the small one around her neck, emphasize Gretchen's simple faith and the danger into which she has fallen.

Plate 11.   NIGHT. STREET BEFORE GRETCHEN'S DOOR. *(Opposite p. 110.)*

> MEPHISTOPHELES: Strike home!
> VALENTINE: Oh!
> MEPHISTOPHELES: Now the fellow's tamed!

Gretchen has at last succumbed to Faust's Devil-aided charms. Valentine, her brother, waits outside her door to avenge her lost honor, as the light of the setting sun slants through the dark streets of the city. Again the approach of night signals the triumph of Mephistopheles' power. At the Devil's urging, Faust runs Valentine through easily, while Mephistopheles effortlessly parries Valentine's thrust. The Devil's lute lies in the street where it fell in the struggle.

Plate 12.   NIGHT. STREET BEFORE GRETCHEN'S DOOR.

> MEPHISTOPHELES:
> Now let's be off! We've got to get out of here!

This plate, which in the 1828 edition immediately follows Plate 11 without any intervening text, depicts the very next moment, as Faust and Mephistopheles flee the scene. The sun has set, and a deep darkness envelops everything. The Devil, as he pulls Faust away, looks over his shoulder toward the dying man on the ground. Martha and Gretchen have found Valentine, and a passerby holds a candle aloft for light. The horror-stricken woman with her hands before her face is undoubtedly Gretchen. The Devil has simply tucked his sword under his right arm in his hurry to escape. Once again, Delacroix has presented a perspective that allows the viewer a unified impression in time of a scene that is presented only sequentially in the text. The device of two illustrations following immediately one upon the other is highly unusual in the nineteenth century, and is reminiscent of twentieth-century experiments with textless "picture novels."

Plate 13.   CATHEDRAL. *(Opposite p. 112.)*

> GRETCHEN:
> Alas, alas,
> Were I but free
> Of these obsessive thoughts
> Which turn against me! . . .
>
> THE EVIL SPIRIT:
> The wrath of God's upon you!
> The trumpets of judgment sound! . . .
> Woe unto you!
>
> THE CHOIR:
> Judex ergo cum sedebit,
> Quidquid latet adparebit,
> Nil inultum remanebit.

Pointing upward toward the wrath of heaven, the Devil torments Gretchen at Mass, reminding her incessantly of her responsibility for the death of both her brother and her mother, and of the fruit of her sin, now taking life within her. To her torment is added the words of the choir: "Lo! he takes his seat of light: / All that's dark shall leap to light, / Guilt, the sword of vengeance smite." Of the many faces Mephistopheles assumes, this is perhaps his most frightening and repellent. Indeed he seems to be screaming his taunts in her ear, while the unhearing crowd of worshipers have turned their backs upon her. She is defenseless, and has as much collapsed as knelt in prayer. The theme of temptation implied in the Devil's position behind Gretchen is continued in the following plate, as Mephistopheles pulls Faust into the witches' sabbath.

Plate 14.   WALPURGIS NIGHT. (*Opposite p. 114.*)

> MEPHISTOPHELES:
> At this rate we're still a long way from our goal.

Faust and Mephistopheles are climbing the Blocksberg to watch the witches' sabbath. Delacroix has combined several elements of Goethe's text. Faust has taken the Devil's advice to "catch hold of my coattails" and is being hauled bodily up the mountain, pushing himself along with the walker's traditional knotted stick. The snakes at the base of the tree correspond to "roots which wind out of sand and stone / like snakes stretching forth strange bands / to frighten and ensnare us." Mephistopheles pulls Faust up the cliff just as he wishes to pull him down to damnation. Delacroix has seized upon this moment in the journey and transformed it into a variant of the story of the fall, for the juxtaposition of Devil and snakes cannot fail to remind us of the tree of knowledge—the knowledge for which Faust risks his soul, and of which the Devil had earlier written in the student's book: "And you will be like God, knowing good and evil."

Plate 15.   WALPURGIS NIGHT. (*Opposite p. 123.*)

> MEPHISTOPHELES:
> Don't pay any heed to that! That does no one any
>   good.
> It's but a fantasy, a lifeless image.
> 'T would be an unfortunate encounter:
> Its rigid gaze congeals men's blood,
> And almost turns them into stone;
> You surely know about Medusa.
>
> FAUST:
> Indeed those are the eyes of someone dead,
> Unclosed by any loving hand.
> That's the breast that Gretchen offered me,
> And the sweet body I enjoyed.

This wild and highly dramatic scene seems to have particularly appealed to Delacroix. Faust and the Devil stand upon a knoll in a raging wind. The scene swarms with both living and dead creatures; indeed, the writhing snakes, glowworms and salamanders at Faust's feet are joined by others mentioned only in the French translation (scorpions, lizards and even a lobster). The twisted, crawling demons in the foreground, as well as those dancing in celebration in the far

distance, serve as a context of general terror for one of the emotional high points of *Faust*. Faust sees Gretchen in death, being dragged off by devils and dark hooded figures of the nether world, at her throat "a single small red band, / no broader than a knife's edge." As this vision threatens to move Faust to repentance, Mephistopheles is shown in a rare moment of fear, his hand at his throat. The entire scene is filled with a visionary horror that makes it a fitting visual counterpart to the most famous witches' night in German literature.

Plate 16.   NIGHT. OPEN FIELD. (*Opposite p. 135*).

> FAUST:
> What are they weaving there around the Rabenstein?
>
> MEPHISTOPHELES:
> No telling what they're cooking up.
>
> FAUST:
> They're floating up and down, bending and bowing
>   about.
>
> MEPHISTOPHELES:
> A witches' coven!
>
> FAUST:
> They're sprinkling and hallowing!
>
> MEPHISTOPHELES:
> We're past them now!

This brief scene in *Faust* serves as a premonition of Gretchen's execution. In the background is the Rabenstein, supposed to be a haunted hanging ground. In addition to the shadowy figures around the gallows, Delacroix has added a grinning demon in the left foreground, seemingly emerging from the earth. He also offers a powerful portrayal of two horses in full gallop; the animals seem almost electrified with energy and terror as they race past the gallows. Faust's hat flies off in the wind, but Mephistopheles has resumed his characteristically calm and unruffled pose.

Plate 17.   DUNGEON. (*Opposite p. 140.*)

> FAUST:
> Come to your senses!
> Just one step and you're free!

Delacroix's final illustration portrays Faust torn between the Devil and his desire to save Gretchen. The diagonal composition is clearly a counterpart to that of Plate 14. Mephistopheles again pulls Faust upward in his attempt to control his soul. Gretchen is saved by her ultimate innocence, and now, as in the first scene in which they met (Plate 8), she rejects Faust and delivers herself over to the judgment of heaven. As Faust points toward the Devil and freedom, the light of morning pours in through the barred window. The keys in the Devil's hand are those of the physical dungeon only; Gretchen achieves true salvation only by divine grace. Just as the setting sun of Plate 1 ushered in the Devil's night, the rising sun reveals the light of heaven, and the Devil's judgment, "She is condemned!," is negated by a voice from above: "She's saved!"

This plate is reproduced here with its original facing text page.

Delacroix Lithog.ᵗ

Lith: de C. Motte.

Original frontispiece of the Delacroix *Faust*.

. . . . . . De temps en temps j'aime à voir le vieux Père,
Et je me garde bien de lui rompre en visière. . . . .

Plate 1

Delacroix invt. et Lithog.

Ch. Motte, Impr. Editeur à Paris.

Pauvre crâne vide que me veux tu dire avec ton grincement hideux ?

Plate 2

Delacroix inv.t et Lith.g

Ch. Motte Imp.r Edteur à Paris.

Faust.— Heureux qui peut conserver l'espérance de surnager sur cet océan d'erreurs !.............
.... l'esprit a beau déployer ses ailes, le corps, hélas ! n'en à point à y ajouter .

Plate 3

Delacroix inv.t et Lithog.

Lithog. de Ch. Motte à Paris.

Il grogne et n'ose vous aborder : Il se couche sur le ventre :
il remue la queue . . . .

Plate 4

Délacroix inv.t et Lithog.   Ch. Motte, Imp.r Editeur, à Paris.

Meph : Pourquoi tout ce vacarme ? que demande Monsieur ? qu'y a-t-il pour son service ?

Plate 5

Delacroix inv.t et Lithog: Ch: Motte, Imp.r Editeur, à Paris.

Meph: Ce que vous avez de mieux à faire, c'est de jurer sur la parole du maître.........
          ..... tenez vous en aux mots: vous êtes sur d'entrer par la grande porte au temple de la vérité.

Plate 6

Delacroix inv. et lithog: Ch. Motte, Imp.ᵉ Éditeur à Paris.

— Au feu, à l'aide, l'enfer s'allume.
......— Sorcellerie ! jettez vous sur lui ... son affaire ne sera pas longue.

Plate 7

Delacroix inv.^t et Lithog.

Ch. Motte Imp.^r Éditeur, à Paris

Faust — Ma belle Demoiselle, oseraisje vous offrir mon bras et vous reconduire chez vous ?..

Plate 8

UNE RUE.

FAUST, MARGUERITE passant.

FAUST.

Ma belle, noble demoiselle, oserais-je vous offrir mon bras et vous reconduire chez vous ?

MARGUERITE.

Je ne suis ni belle, ni noble demoiselle, et pour rentrer chez moi je n'ai besoin du bras de personne.

(Elle se débarrasse et s'enfuit.)

FAUST.

Par Dieu, voilà une belle enfant! Je n'ai jamais rien vu de si charmant; il y a en elle tant de modestie et de décence, et en même temps quelque chose de dédaigneux... la rougeur de ses lèvres, l'éclat de ses joues... je ne l'oublierai de ma vie! Ses regards baissés vers la terre se sont gravés profondément dans mon cœur, et sa brusque répartie... C'est à ravir!

(MÉPHISTOPHÉLÈS s'approche.)

FAUST.

Écoute ici. Il faut que tu me procures cette jeune fille.

MÉPHISTOPHÉLÈS.

Laquelle?

FAUST.

Celle qui vient de passer.

MÉPHISTOPHÉLÈS.

Celle-là, dites-vous? Elle venait de chez un prêtre, qui lui a donné l'absolution de tous ses péchés; je m'étais glissé tout près du confessionnal : c'est l'innocence même, elle allait à confesse pour un rien. Je n'ai aucun pouvoir sur elle.

FAUST.

Elle a pourtant plus de quatorze ans.

MÉPHISTOPHÉLÈS.

Tu t'exprimes comme Roger Bontemps, qui veut que toutes les jolies fleurs soient pour lui, et s'imagine qu'honneurs et faveurs, tout est à la portée de sa main : mais il n'en va pas toujours ainsi.

Delacroix inv.t et Lithog:

Lith de l'Motte. a Paris

Meph: Il est bien hardi à moi de m'introduire aussi brusquement chez ces Dames, je leur en
demande un million de pardons..............

Plate 9

Delacroix invt et Lithog: Ch. Motte, Impr Editeur, à Paris.

Sans lui l'existence
N'est qu'un lourd fardeau
Ce monde si beau
N'est qu'un tombeau
Dans son absence.

Plate 10

Delacroix inv.t et lithog.

Ch. Motte, Imp.r Editeur à Paris.

Meph. — Pousse .. Val — of ! .... Meph. — Voilà mon rustaud apprivoisé !

Plate 11

Delacroix inv.^t et Lithog: Ch. Motte Imp.^r Editeur a Paris

Meph:— Il nous faut gagner promptement au large.

Plate 12

Delacroix inv.ᵗ et Lithog:

Ch. Motte, Impʳ Editeur, à Paris

Marg.— Malheureuse ! ah ! si je pouvais me soustraire aux pensées qui se succèdent en tumulte dans mon âme et s'élèvent contre moi
Le mauvais Esprit.— La colère de Dieu tombe sur toi ! la trompette sonne..... Malheur à toi .
Chœur.— Judex ergo cùm sedebit ,
Quid quid latet apparebit .
Nil multum remanebit .

Plate 13

Delacroix inv.t et Lithog: Ch: Motte, Imp.t Editeur, a Paris.

Meph. — Nous sommes encore loin du terme de notre course

Plate 14

Plate 15

Delacroix inv.t et lithp.

J. Motte, Imp.r Editeur, à Paris.

Faust. — Que vois-je remuer autour de ce gibet ?...............

— ..... ils vont et viennent, ils se baissent et se relèvent .

Meph. — C'est une assemblée de Sorciers .

Plate 16

MARGUERITE.

Laisse-moi! Non, je ne souffrirai point la violence; ne porte pas sur moi tes mains meurtrières, ne me saisis pas ainsi!..... Souviens-toi que j'ai tout fait pour te plaire.

FAUST.

Le jour paraît. Mon amie, ma douce amie!

MARGUERITE.

Le jour?..... Oui, il fait jour; mon dernier jour pénètre ici..... Ce devait être mon jour de noces!..... Ne dis à personne, au moins, que tu étais déja près de Marguerite..... Oh! ma guirlande, où est-elle?.... Nous nous reverrons, mais non pas au bal..... La foule se presse, et on ne l'entend pas; la place, les rues ne peuvent la contenir; la cloche sonne, le signal est donné [44]... Comme ils me prennent et m'enchaînent! Me voici déja montée sur l'échafaud, déja tombe sur le cou de chacun des spectateurs le tranchant qui s'abat sur le mien..... Le monde est muet comme un tombeau.

FAUST.

Ah! pourquoi suis-je né?

(MÉPHISTOPHÉLÈS se montre à la porte.)

MÉPHISTOPHÉLÈS.

Hors d'ici, ou vous êtes perdus. Que de paroles inutiles, que de délais et d'incertitudes! Mes chevaux frissonnent, l'aube blanchit l'horizon.

MARGUERITE.

Qui s'élève de terre?..... C'est lui! C'est lui! Chassez-le. Que veut-il dans le saint lieu?..... Il veut mon ame!

FAUST.

Il faut absolument que tu vives.

MARGUERITE.

Justice de Dieu, je me suis abandonnée à toi.

MÉPHISTOPHÉLÈS à Faust.

Viens toi-même, ou je te laisse avec elle sous le couteau.

MARGUERITE.

Je suis à toi, Père céleste! Anges, déployez vos saintes armées, protégez-moi..... Henri, tu me fais horreur!

MÉPHISTOPHÉLÈS.

Elle est jugée.

Delacroix inv. et Lithog.   Imp. Bertauts à Paris.

Faust. __Reviens à toi ! un seul pas et tu es libre . . .
Meph. . . . . Que de paroles inutiles ! que de délais et d'incertitudes !
            mes chevaux frissonnent : l'aube blanchit l'horizon .

Plate 17

Notes on the Plates for "The Raven"

The illustrations for *The Raven* consist of a frontispiece (the raven's head) and an ex libris (the raven in flight), as well as four illustrations proper to the poem itself. Manet utilized a technique called transfer lithography in these plates. He painted with a brush on moisture-repellent paper; the image was then transferred to the lithographic stone by pressure. The plates that were subsequently pulled from the stone bear the exact image of the original drawing. By contrast, Delacroix's lithographs, which he prepared directly upon the stone, produced images that are the reverse of what he saw on the stone's surface. Both methods, of course, result in equally original works of art.

The juxtaposition of Manet's illustrations with those of Delacroix is an illuminating one. One can easily see, for example, that the number of plates in the series is determined to a great extent by the text to be illustrated—we would hardly have expected seventeen illustrations for a poem printed on four pages (in each language). In *The Raven*, each of the four full-page illustrations is carefully balanced by a single page of English text, with the equivalent paragraphs of Mallarmé's prose translation on the right-hand page immediately following. Like Delacroix, it is evident that Manet was thoroughly familiar with his text, and the reader has no trouble identifying the relevant passage for each illustration. In spite of the total disparity of texts, certain similarities are immediately evident. Night dominates both works, as well as a visitor from the realm of darkness ("thing of evil—prophet still, if bird or devil!"), from whom a melancholy and resigned man seeks knowledge. Although such similarities are superficial ones, they do serve to indicate why black-and-white lithography seems appropriate in each case; the mood of Faust in his study is not, after all, that far removed from that of the man at his desk in *The Raven*, pondering over "many a quaint and curious volume of forgotten lore."

In most respects, of course, the plates are strikingly dissimilar. Manet has created a series of studies in which a sense of stasis is pervasive. Even the second illustration, in which the raven enters "with many a flirt and flutter," seems frozen in time, while the psychological tension is focused within a startled, rigid hand. So too in the first illustration it is the turn of a head, at the motionless moment of listening, that seizes the mood. Where, in *Faust*, Delacroix's love of motion is often in evidence, it is formal characteristics that provide a sense of excitement in *The Raven*: the sharp tilt upward induced in the third illustration, in which the bust of Pallas beneath the raven is suddenly and surprisingly reflected by the truncated head and shoulders of the man below; or the final illustration, surely the most daring of nineteenth-century book illustrations, in which only the shadow of living substance remains.

ex libris

LE CORBEAU

LE
CORBEAU

THE RAVEN

POËME

PAR

EDGAR POE

TRADUCTION FRANÇAISE DE STÉPHANE MALLARMÉ

AVEC ILLUSTRATIONS

PAR

ÉDOUARD MANET

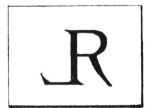

PARIS

RICHARD LESCLIDE, ÉDITEUR, 61, RUE DE LAFAYETTE

———

1875

N° 219

Stéphane Mallarmé.

E Manet

LE CORBEAU

THE RAVEN

ONCE upon a midnight dreary, while I pondered, weak and weary,
Over many a quaint and curious volume of forgotten lore —
While I nodded, nearly napping, suddenly there came a tapping,
As of some one gently rapping — rapping at my chamber door.
" 'T is some visitor, " I muttered, " tapping at my chamber door —
                    Only this and nothing more. "

Ah, distinctly I remember, it was in the bleak December,
And each separate dying ember wrought its ghost upon the floor.
Eagerly I wished the morrow ; — vainly I had sought to borrow
From my books surcease of sorrow — sorrow for the lost Lenore —
For the rare and radiant maiden whom the angels name Lenore —
                    Nameless here for evermore.

And the silken sad uncertain rustling of each purple curtain
Thrilled me — filled me with fantastic terrors never felt before ;
So that now, to still the beating of my heart, I stood repeating
" 'T is some visitor entreating entrance at my chamber door —
Some late visitor entreating entrance at my chamber door ; —
                    This it is and nothing more. "

Presently my soul grew stronger ; hesitating then no longer,
" Sir, " said I, " or Madam, truly your forgiveness I implore ;
But the fact is I was napping, and so gently you came rapping,
And so faintly you came tapping — tapping at my chamber door,
That I scarce was sure I heard you " — here I opened wide the door : —
                    Darkness there and nothing more.

Une fois, par un minuit lugubre, tandis que je m'appesantissais, faible et fatigué, sur maint curieux et bizarre volume de savoir oublié — tandis que je dodelinais la tête, somnolant presque : soudain se fit un heurt, comme de quelqu'un frappant doucement, frappant à la porte de ma chambre — cela seul et rien de plus.

Ah ! distinctement je me souviens que c'était en le glacial Décembre : et chaque tison, mourant isolé, ouvrageait son spectre sur le sol. Ardemment je souhaitais le jour — vainement j'avais cherché d'emprunter à mes livres un sursis au chagrin — au chagrin de la Lénore perdue — de la rare et rayonnante jeune fille que les anges nomment Lénore : — de nom pour elle ici, non, jamais plus !

Et de la soie l'incertain et triste bruissement en chaque rideau purpural me traversait — m'emplissait de fantastiques terreurs pas senties encore : si bien que, pour calmer le battement de mon cœur, je demeurais maintenant à répéter « C'est quelque visiteur qui sollicite l'entrée, à la porte de ma chambre — quelque visiteur qui sollicite l'entrée, à la porte de ma chambre ; c'est cela et rien de plus. »

Mon âme devint subitement plus forte et, n'hésitant davantage « Monsieur, dis-je, ou Madame, j'implore véritablement votre pardon ; mais le fait est que je somnolais et vous vîntes si doucement frapper, et si faiblement vous vîntes heurter, heurter à la porte de ma chambre, que j'étais à peine sûr de vous avoir entendu. » — Ici j'ouvris, grande, la porte : les ténèbres et rien de plus. »

Deep into that darkness peering, long I stood there wondering, fearing,

Doubting, dreaming dreams no mortal ever dared to dream before;

But the silence was unbroken, and the stillness gave no token,

And the only word there spoken was the whispered word, " Lenore ! "

This I whispered, and an echo murmured back the word, " Lenore ! " —

Merely this and nothing more.

Back into the chamber turning, all my soul within me burning,

Soon again I heard a tapping, somewhat louder than before,

" Surely, " said I, " surely that is something at my window lattice;

Let me see, then, what thereat is, and this mystery explore —

Let my heart be still a moment, and this mystery explore; —

'T is the wind and nothing more. "

Open here I flung the shutter, when, with many a flirt and flutter,

In there stepped a stately Raven of the saintly days of yore.

Not the least obeisance made he; not an instant stopped or stayed he;

But, with mien of lord and lady, perched above my chamber door —

Perched upon a bust of Pallas just above my chamber door —

Perched and sat and nothing more.

Then this ebony bird beguiling my sad fancy into smiling,

By the grave and stern decorum of the countenance it wore,

" Though thy crest be shorn and shaven, thou, " I said, " art sure no craven,

Ghastly grim and ancient Raven wandering from the Nightly shore —

Tell me what thy lordly name is on the Night's Plutonian shore ! "

Quoth the Raven, " Nevermore. "

Much I marvelled this ungainly fowl to hear discourse so plainly,

Though its answer little meaning — little relevancy bore;

For we cannot help agreeing that no living human being

Ever yet was blessed with seeing bird above his chamber door —

Bird or beast upon the sculptured bust above his chamber door,

With such a name as " Nevermore. "

Loin dans l'ombre regardant, je me tins longtemps à douter, m'étonner et craindre, à rêver des rêves qu'aucun mortel n'avait osé rêver encore ; mais le silence ne se rompit point et la quiétude ne donna de signe : et le seul mot qui se dit, fut le mot chuchoté « Lénore ! » Je le chuchotai — et un écho murmura de retour le mot « Lénore ! » — purement cela et rien de plus.

Rentrant dans la chambre, toute mon âme en feu, j'entendis bientôt un heurt en quelque sorte plus fort qu'auparavant. « Sûrement, dis-je, sûrement c'est quelque chose à la persienne de ma fenêtre. Voyons donc ce qu'il y a et explorons ce mystère — que mon cœur se calme un moment et explore ce mystère ; c'est le vent et rien de plus. »

Au large je poussai le volet ; quand, avec maints enjouement et agitation d'ailes, entra un majestueux Corbeau des saints jours de jadis. Il ne fit pas la moindre révérence, il ne s'arrêta ni n'hésita un instant : mais, avec une mine de lord ou de lady, se percha au-dessus de la porte de ma chambre — se percha sur un buste de Pallas juste au-dessus de la porte de ma chambre — se percha, siégea et rien de plus.

Alors cet oiseau d'ébène induisant ma triste imagination au sourire, par le grave et sévère décorum de la contenance qu'il eut : « Quoique ta crête soit chue et rase, non ! dis-je, tu n'es pas pour sûr un poltron, spectral, lugubre et ancien Corbeau, errant loin du rivage de Nuit — dis-moi quel est ton nom seigneurial au rivage plutonien de Nuit. » Le Corbeau dit : « Jamais plus. »

Je m'émerveillai fort d'entendre ce disgracieux volatile s'énoncer aussi clairement, quoique sa réponse n'eût que peu de sens et peu d'à-propos ; car on ne peut s'empêcher de convenir que nul homme vivant n'eût encore l'heur de voir un oiseau au-dessus de la porte de sa chambre — un oiseau ou toute autre bête sur le buste sculpté, au-dessus de la porte de sa chambre, avec un nom tel que : « Jamais plus. »

But the Raven, sitting lonely on that placid bust, spoke only
That one word, as if his soul in that one word he did outpour.
Nothing further then he uttered; not a feather then he fluttered —
Till I scarcely more than muttered, " Other friends have flown before —
On the morrow *he* will leave me, as my Hopes have flown before."
                    Then the bird said, " Nevermore."

Startled at the stillness broken by reply so aptly spoken,
" Doubtless," said I, " what it utters is its only stock and store,
Caught from some unhappy master, whom unmerciful Disaster
Followed fast and followed faster till his songs one burden bore —
Till the dirges of his Hope the melancholy burden bore
                    Of ' Never — nevermore.' "

But the Raven still beguiling all my sad soul into smiling,
Straight I wheeled a cushioned seat in front of bird and bust and door;
Then, upon the velvet sinking, I betook myself to linking
Fancy unto fancy, thinking what this ominous bird of yore —
What this grim, ungainly, ghastly, gaunt and ominous bird of yore
                    Meant in croaking " Nevermore."

This I sat engaged in guessing, but no syllable expressing
To the fowl whose fiery eyes now burned into my bosom's core;
This and more I sat divining, with my head at ease reclining
On the cushion's velvet lining that the lamp-light gloated o'er,
But whose velvet violet lining with the lamp-light gloating o'er,
                    She shall press, ah, nevermore! ·

Then, methought, the air grew denser, perfumed from an unseen censer,
Swung by Seraphim whose foot-falls tinkled on the tufted floor.
" Wretch," I cried, " thy God hath lent thee — by these angels he hath sent thee
Respite — respite and nepenthe from thy memories of Lenore!
Quaff, oh quaff this kind nepenthe, and forget this lost Lenore!"
                    Quoth the Raven, " Nevermore."

Mais le Corbeau, perché solitairement sur ce buste placide, parla ce seul mot comme si, son âme, en ce seul mot, il la répandait. Je ne proférai donc rien de plus : il n'agita donc pas de plume — jusqu'à ce que je fis à peine davantage que marmotter « D'autres amis déjà ont pris leur vol — demain il me laissera comme mes Espérances déjà ont pris leur vol. » Alors l'oiseau dit : « Jamais plus. »

Tressaillant au calme rompu par une réplique si bien parlée : « Sans doute, dis-je, ce qu'il profère est tout son fonds et son bagage, pris à quelque malheureux maître que l'impitoyable Désastre suivit de près et de très-près suivit jusqu'à ce que ses chansons comportassent un unique refrain ; jusqu'à ce que les chants funèbres de son Espérance comportassent le mélancolique refrain de « Jamais — jamais plus. »

Le Corbeau induisant toute ma triste âme encore au sourire, je roulai soudain un siège à coussins en face de l'oiseau et du buste et de la porte ; et m'enfonçant dans le velours, je me pris à enchaîner songerie à songerie, pensant à ce que cet augural oiseau de jadis — à ce que ce sombre, disgracieux, sinistre, maigre et augural oiseau de jadis signifiait en croassant : « Jamais plus. »

Cela, je m'assis occupé à le conjecturer, mais n'adressant pas une syllabe à l'oiseau dont les yeux de feu brûlaient, maintenant, au fond de mon sein ; cela et plus encore, je m'assis pour le deviner, ma tête reposant à l'aise sur la housse de velours des coussins que dévorait la lumière de la lampe, housse violette de velours dévoré par la lumière de la lampe qu'Elle ne pressera plus, ah ! jamais plus.

L'air, me sembla-t-il, devint alors plus dense, parfumé selon un encensoir invisible balancé par les Séraphins dont le pied, dans sa chute, tintait sur l'étoffe du parquet. « Misérable, m'écriai-je, ton Dieu t'a prêté — il t'a envoyé, par ces anges, le répit — le répit et le népenthès dans ta mémoire de Lénore ! Bois ! oh ! bois ce bon népenthès et oublie cette Lénore perdue ! » Le Corbeau dit : « Jamais plus ! »

" Prophet! " said I, " thing of evil! — prophet still, if bird or devil! —
Whether Tempter sent, or whether tempest tossed thee here ashore,
Desolate yet all undaunted, on this desert land enchanted —
On this home by Horror haunted — tell me truly, I implore —
Is there — *is* there balm in Gilead? — tell me — tell me I implore! "
                                        Quoth the Raven, " Nevermore. "

" Prophet! " said I, " thing of evil! — prophet still, if bird or devil!
By that Heaven that bends above us — by that God we both adore —
Tell this soul with sorrow laden if, within the distant Aidenn,
It shall clasp a saintly maiden whom the angels name Lenore —
Clasp a rare and radiant maiden whom the angels name Lenore. "
                                        Quoth the Raven, " Nevermore. "

" Be that word our sign of parting, bird or fiend! " I shrieked, upstarting —
" Get thee back into the tempest and the Night's Plutonian shore!
Leave no black plume as a token of that lie thy soul hath spoken!
Leave my loneliness unbroken! — quit the bust above my door!
Take thy beak from out my heart, and take thy form from off my door! "
                                        Quoth the Raven, " Nevermore. "

And the Raven, never flitting, still is sitting — still is sitting
On the pallid bust of Pallas juste above my chamber door ;
And his eyes have all the seeming of a Demon's that is dreaming,
And the lamp-light o'er him streaming throws his shadow on the floor;
And my soul from out that shadow that lies floating on the floor
                                        Shall be lifted — nevermore!

« *Prophète, dis-je, être de malheur ! prophète, oui, oiseau ou démon ! Que si le Tentateur t'envoya ou la tempête t'échoua vers ces bords, désolé et encore tout indompté, vers cette déserte terre enchantée — vers ce logis par l'horreur hanté : dis-moi véritablement, je t'implore ! y a-t-il du baume en Judée ? — dis-moi, je t'implore.* » *Le Corbeau dit :* « *Jamais plus !* »

« *Prophète, dis-je, être de malheur ! prophète, oui, oiseau ou démon ! Par les Cieux sur nous épars — et le Dieu que nous adorons tous deux — dis à cette âme de chagrin chargée si, dans le distant Eden, elle doit embrasser une jeune fille sanctifiée que les anges nomment Lénore — embrasser une rare et rayonnante jeune fille que les anges nomment Lénore.* » *Le Corbeau dit :* « *Jamais plus !* »

« *Que ce mot soit le signal de notre séparation, oiseau ou malin esprit,* » *hurlai-je, en me dressant.* « *Recule en la tempête et le rivage plutonien de Nuit ! Ne laisse pas une plume noire ici comme un gage du mensonge qu'a proféré ton âme. Laisse inviolé mon abandon ! quitte le buste au-dessus de ma porte ! ôte ton bec de mon cœur et jette ta forme loin de ma porte !* » *Le Corbeau dit :* « *Jamais plus !* »

Et le Corbeau, sans voleter, siége encore — siége encore sur le buste pallide de Pallas, juste au-dessus de la porte de ma chambre, et ses yeux ont toute la semblance des yeux d'un démon qui rêve, et la lumière de la lampe, ruisselant sur lui, projette son ombre à terre : et mon âme, de cette ombre qui gît flottante à terre, ne s'élèvera — jamais plus !

ACHEVÉ D'IMPRIMER

LE VINGT MAI MIL HUIT CENT SOIXANTE-QUINZE

PAR ALCAN LÉVY, A PARIS.